LISTEN
TO THE
TREES

MOLLY CONE

LISTEN
TO THE
TREES

Jews and the Earth

Illustrations by
ROY DOTY

UAHC PRESS ✦ NEW YORK

To my husband, our children,
and our children's children
Molly Cone

To Rachel and Michael
Roy Doty

Library of Congress Cataloging-in-Publication Data

Cone, Molly.
Listen to the trees : Jews and the earth /
Molly Cone ; illustrated by Roy Doty.
p.   cm.
Includes bibliographical references.
ISBN 0-8074-0536-1 : $14.95
1. Human ecology—Religious aspects—Judaism—
Juvenile literature.
I. Doty, Roy, 1922—   ill.   II. Title.
BM538.H85C66   1995
296.3'878362—dc20   95-5016
                                       CIP
                                        AC

Photo Credits
Israel Ministry of Tourism, pp. 2, 16, 28, 64
Israel Press and Photo Agency, p. 46

This book is printed on acid-free paper
Copyright © 1995 by Molly Cone
Manufactured in the United States of America
10   9   8   7   6   5   4   3   2   1

Feldman Library

THE FELDMAN LIBRARY FUND was created in 1974 through a gift from the Milton and Sally Feldman Foundation. The Feldman Library Fund, which provides for the publication by the UAHC of selected outstanding Jewish books and texts, memorializes Sally Feldman, who in her lifetime devoted herself to Jewish youth and Jewish learning. Herself an orphan and brought up in an orphanage, she dedicated her efforts to helping Jewish young people get the educational opportunities she had not enjoyed.

In loving memory of my beloved wife Sally
''She was my life, and she is gone;
She was my riches, and I am a pauper.''

''Many daughters have done valiantly,
but thou excellest them all.''

Milton E. Feldman

Contents

IV

Torah says:
Do not destroy.

V

Torah says:
All living things are connected.

Introduction

A long long time ago—before there were people, before there were trees and flowers and plants, before there were fish in the sea and birds in the air, and before there were spiders and frogs and alligators and elephants—there was Earth, slowly revolving around the sun.

On Earth there were lands and seas and not much else—until life began.

First came plants and trees, then came fish and birds and mammals—and finally came human beings.

All were living things. And all living things were dependent on one another. They were connected, like a family is connected, one to the other. Although they did not know it, they were bound to one another, like the silky strands in a spider's web and the links in an endless chain.

The story of the world that God created is told in the Torah, the first five books of the Bible. The Torah also tells us how to protect and preserve the earth and all the living things that dwell on it.

Early rabbis recited the words of the Torah, the Five Books of Moses, over and over again. They explained the Torah's meaning through stories gathered in collections called the Midrash. The interpretations of the laws and teachings of the Torah were recorded in a great collection of books called the Talmud.

In the writings of the Midrash and the Talmud, some of the words of the Torah were changed to make their meaning clear. In this book, *Listen to the Trees,* some of the words of the Torah have been simplified to help you understand them better. Every time these words are quoted, they are followed by the original source.

The Torah includes directions on planting and harvesting, caring and feeding of animals, and maintaining the health of the land as well as that of the community.

Among these is the law *Bal Tashchit,* "Do Not Destroy." It is prohibited to cut down fruit-bearing trees, to plug up a spring, to pile up wastes near a dwelling, and to let grapes wither on the vine. The Torah tells people to waste nothing—not even a small mustard seed.

That such modern ideas about the environment are part of a religion as ancient as Judaism may surprise many people but not those who study the Jewish religion. After you read this book, you will not be surprised, either.

LISTEN
TO THE
TREES

I ✦

Torah says:

Care for
the trees.

Your life and the lives of all the people on the earth depend on trees.

For hundreds of years, rabbis have taught that planting trees preserves the earth and all who live on it. Trees provide food for living creatures. They benefit the air, soil, and water of the land. Trees regulate climate, protect water supplies, and nurture millions of species of animals. From trees and other plants come more than half of the medicines known to humankind. Tu Bishvat is a Jewish festival for honoring trees. On this holiday, tree-planting ceremonies are held by Jews throughout the world.

✦ ✦ ✦

Even if the land is full of all good things, still you must plant . . . even if you are old, you must plant. Just as you found trees planted by others, you must plant them for your children. (*Midrash Tanchuma, Kodashim* 8)

It was an old Jewish custom to plant a cedar tree when a boy was born and a pine tree when a girl was born. When two people married, a wedding canopy was made from the branches. (Babylonian Talmud, *Gittin* 57a)

4

In Judaism the Torah is known as the Tree of Life. (Proverbs 3:18) Like a tree that makes life better for everything around it, the Torah makes life better for all who learn from it.

If not for the trees, human life could not exist. (*Midrash Sifre* to Deuteronomy 20:19)

Rabbi Yohanan ben Zakkai used to say: "If you have a sapling in your hand and you are told that the Messiah has come, first plant the sapling and then go welcome the Messiah." (*Avot de-Rabbi Natan* 31b)

It is forbidden to live in a town in which there is no garden or greenery. (Jerusalem Talmud, *Kodashim* 4:12)

If a man kills a tree before its time, it is as though he has murdered a soul. (Rabbi Nachman of Bratzlav)

One who buys a tree from a friend for felling shall cut it in such a way that the stump remains from which a new tree can grow. (Babylonian Talmud, *Baba Batra* 80b)

The Old Man
and the Pear Tree

A young rider stopped to watch a very old man planting a pear tree. The old man's hands shook as he dug a hole. His old legs trembled and the air wheezed in and out of his chest with his every movement.

"Hey, old man!" called out the rider. "Isn't it a bit foolish to work so hard planting a tree that won't bear fruit for many years?"

The old man raised his eyes from his planting. "Foolish?" he repeated in a quavering voice.

"You plan to live long enough to eat the fruit from this tree?" The rider burst out laughing.

The old man looked down at his old legs, which had carried him for almost a hundred years. Then he looked at the spindly roots of the young tree. The fruit from this tree will be truly fine, he thought.

"No, I won't be here to eat the pears that this tree will produce," he said aloud to the rider. Then he smiled happily. "But my grandchildren will."

And he went back to his work.

(Based on a story in the Babylonian Talmud, *Ta'anit* 23a)

When the Trees Talked

It is said that in the Garden of Eden, the trees could talk and the flowers could sing. But that was a long, long time ago. It was so long ago that no one can tell you whether this is still so. No one, that is, except a storyteller.

A tale is told of an old woman who had lost her way in a forest while picking mushrooms. The trees were many, the forest was deep, the path was narrow and winding, and the mushrooms were few and far between.

Before the old woman knew it, the path had disappeared, the sun was setting, and darkness was creeping all around her. Anxiously she hurried in one direction and then another, but neither led her out of the dense woods.

"Oh dear, oh dear," she muttered to herself, trying to stay calm. She leaned against a tree, took a deep breath, and tried to think what to do. But all she could think of were the terrible things that could happen to a person who is lost and alone in the cold woods at night. Had she not warned her own daughters and sons of this very danger?

They were all grown up now. The only one who lived with her was the boy who chopped the wood and weeded the garden. At the thought of the boy, she stopped worrying about herself and began to worry about him.

If she didn't find her way out soon, there would be no supper on the table for him and there would be no one to help him with his lessons.

She thought of praying but she had gotten out of the habit, and it seemed silly to stand in the middle of a forest and talk to someone she could not see. But as darkness fell, she decided she would try to pray.

She tied her scarf more neatly around her head, brushed the leaves and twigs from her skirt, and laid her hand against the rough trunk of a tree to steady herself.

"Oh, please," she said, "help me find my way back."

"This way," said a soft voice beside her.

She looked all around but saw only the tree against which she was leaning. She took a few steps forward and laid her hand on the tree trunk in front of her.

"This way," she heard once again.

Tree by tree, she moved along, hearing "this way" repeated many times.

When she finally reached the edge of the forest and saw the

road that led to her little house with its flowers blooming in the window boxes, she sat down and cried.

"How did you find your way out?" asked the boy, as she was serving him the hot mushroom soup she had made.

"The trees talked to me," she answered.

The boy stopped eating. His spoon seemed to be stuck in the air. For just one moment he thought he heard the flowers singing.

(Based on a legend of unknown origin)

The Two Scholars

Samuel and Nathan were scholars. They were also neighbors and rivals. Samuel prided himself on studying from early in the morning until late at night. He stopped only for prayers and to observe the holy days and the festivals.

Every Sabbath he said a special prayer to God. He was always careful to point out what a diligent student he was, how worthy and how holy. He was a cautious man. It was never too early, he believed, to prepare a welcome for himself in the next world. Then he would eat his Sabbath dinner with a good appetite and go to bed.

Nathan was also an earnest student, but he regularly set his books aside to tend to his garden. Each year he carefully pruned the apple and cherry trees he had planted around his house. He watered the earth often and spent many hours planting flowers and pulling up weeds. Every Sabbath he would rest and look out with pleasure upon the growing trees and flowers. Every spring he would take time from his studies to gaze upon the cherry and apple blossoms and the first blooming flowers and to thank God for bringing him to this day on which he could enjoy the beauty of God's world.

When the end of days came for Samuel and Nathan, they

found themselves standing together before the door of the House of God.

"The one who has been the more holy in his life on the earth will be the first to enter," announced an angel. Confident of his superiority, Samuel brushed the last of the earth's dust from his trousers and rebuttoned his jacket.

The angel brought out the great book of records that would be presented to God. "Each of you will bear witness for the other," she said. She turned first to Nathan.

Nathan told her that Samuel had never forgotten to observe a holy day or festival, that he had studied night and day and had never let anything interfere with his studies.

She wrote down every word in the great book and then turned to Samuel.

Confident that his neighbor's report of his studious habits would surely impress God, Samuel conscientiously pointed out that although Nathan had been an equally good—well almost an equally good—student, he had often put aside his books to plant flowers and to sit under his fruit trees.

Then Samuel stood ready to be chosen to enter the House of God first.

But lo, the door swung open first not for Samuel, the righteous and diligent student, but for Nathan, the tree and flower planter.

(Based on a Jewish legend)

The world is a tree and
human beings its fruit.
(Rabbi Solomon ibn Gabirol,
Malaga, Spain)

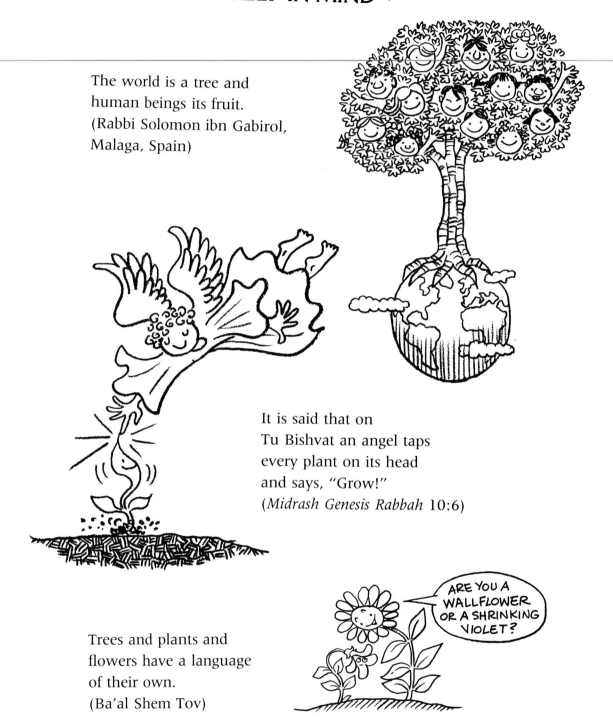

It is said that on
Tu Bishvat an angel taps
every plant on its head
and says, "Grow!"
(*Midrash Genesis Rabbah* 10:6)

Trees and plants and
flowers have a language
of their own.
(Ba'al Shem Tov)

14

Long, long ago it was the custom for a Jewish woman who wanted a baby to plant raisins and candy under a tree on Tu Bishvat.

It is said that all trees embrace on Tu Bishvat. And if you are lucky enough to witness this miraculous event, your wish will come true.

The almond tree has a special significance on Tu Bishvat. The word for almond in Hebrew means to "watch" or "wake." The almond tree is among the first to awaken from its winter sleep. The almond tree celebrates the fifteenth of Shevat in full blossom.

II ✦

Torah says:

Care for
the birds,
the beasts,
and the fish.

All breathing things that fly, run, swim, slither, or creep are part of the world in which you live.

There is a saying in Hebrew, "Tza'ar Ba'alei Chayim," which means "Compassion toward All Living Creatures." Consideration for animals is so much a part of Judaism that the Fourth Commandment states that the animals of one's household must rest on the Sabbath along with the members of the family.

✦   ✦   ✦

Do not buy an animal before buying food for that animal to eat. (Jerusalem Talmud, *Ketubot* 4:8)

You must not sit down to your own meal before you have fed your pets and barnyard animals. (Babylonian Talmud, *Berachot* 40a based on Deuteronomy 11:15)

Do not take the mother bird together with her young or her eggs.
(Deuteronomy 22:6–7)

To kill a mother bird and her babies threatens the survival of that species.
(Nachmanides, Barcelona, Spain, 1194–1270 C.E.)

A young domestic animal must not be separated from its mother until it is at least seven days old.
(Leviticus 22:27)

If you see someone's animal wandering off, bring it back, even if it belongs to your enemy. (Exodus 23:4) If you see the donkey of your enemy suffering under a too heavy load, you must help it. (Exodus 23:5)

Killing an animal for sport is against Jewish law. (*Avodah Zarah* 18b) When an animal must be killed for food, it must be done in such a way that the pain to the animal is as little as possible. (Babylonian Talmud, *Baba Metzia* 31a–32b) This is the reason why some Jewish people eat only kosher meat. Kosher meat is slaughtered by a *shochet*. A *shochet* is skilled in slaughtering animals for food in the least painful way.

Right-minded people have regard for the lives of their animals. (Proverbs 12:10) A good person does not sell an animal to a cruel person.

19

The Rooster

A rabbi invited three men from his congregation to accompany him to the country and help him put up a new roof on a poor woman's house.

After a long and tiring ride in a horse-drawn wagon that rattled and bounced over rutted roads, the four men arrived and immediately set to work. They worked long into the evening, stopping only for a scant supper before returning to their task.

They hammered in the last nail by the waning light of the moon, wearily rolled themselves into blankets, and fell asleep. They had hardly closed their eyes when they were abruptly awakened by the crowing of a rooster.

"Cock-a-dooooooooodle dooooooooooooooooo!"

Muttering, the three tired workers pulled their blankets over their ears and tried to go back to sleep. But sleep was impossible.

"Cock-a-dooooooooodle dooooooooooooooooo!"

"Shut up!" they shouted. One flung a shoe in the direction from which the sound was coming.

The rooster crowed again.

Wide awake now, the men groaned.

The rabbi sat up and yawned. "Look at that," he said, pointing to the rising sun.

The men gazed at the dark sky that was taking on a pink

glow. As dawn broke over the land, dew shimmered on the grass and leaves and birds began to sing.

The rabbi flung back his blanket, stood up, and headed for the lake to dip his head into the water. The men followed, grumbling and cursing the rooster.

In the morning light the leaves on the trees sparkled with dew. Tiny wild strawberries peeked out from vines creeping along the ground. The fragrance of the flowers mingled with the scent of the green grass and ripening fruit.

"I think we should take a moment to give thanks to the Creator," the rabbi said.

His companions dutifully bowed their heads.

"Praise to God who created the beauty of the sunrise," began the rabbi.

"Amen," said the three.

"Praise to God whose creation brought forth the song of the birds."

21

"Amen," they repeated.

"Praise to God for the beauty of the morning."

"Amen," they said.

"And finally," the rabbi said solemnly, "praise to God for roosters."

"Roosters!" exclaimed the three.

"Without the crowing of the rooster," said the rabbi, "would we have seen the colors of the sunrise? Or heard the first song of the birds? Or witnessed such a beautiful morning?"

For a moment the three helpers were silent. Then they mumbled dutifully, "Praise to God for roosters."

And the rabbi replied, "Amen."

The Challenge

He was the biggest man in town. Everyone called him Champ.

He wore so many first-place medals that he clanked with every step he took. So impressed was he with his own size and accomplishments that he offered a bag of gold to anyone living on God's earth who could prove to be more important than he was.

No one appeared at his door to try for the prize—except for a flea.

"A flea?" The great man snorted. "My challenge has been accepted by a *flea*!" And he laughed so hard that his aides had to throw a pail of water on him to prevent him from laughing himself to death.

On the day of the contest, all the people living in or near the town gathered. The street was crowded with men, women, children, dogs, cats, squirrels, birds, and even frogs and snakes. Everyone wanted to witness the event.

"So what do you have to say for yourself?" the important man boomed at the tiny creature.

"Only this," said the flea. "Tell me: How long did it take God to create the world?"

Champ laughed. "Why you insignificant little creature—seven days, of course."

"What came first in Creation?" asked the flea.

Champ promptly answered, "Day and night!"

"And what came next?"

"The land and the waters," Champ said, smiling. "And after that came the plants and the trees. And then came the birds of the air, the beasts, the fish, and all the creeping things of the earth . . ."

"And what came last in Creation?" asked the flea.

"Man!" answered Champ proudly, drawing himself up to his full stature and looking out upon the crowd like a king reviewing his subjects.

"Aha!" said the flea triumphantly. "If you came last, then I came *before* you in Creation. So *I* am more important than you are!"

And all the fleas in the town swarmed down on the defeated Champ to claim the bag of gold.

(Based on a quotation from the Babylonian Talmud, *Sanhedrin* 38a)

✦ KEEP IN MIND ✦

Throwing stones at a dog or cat or hurting an animal in any way is against Jewish law. (Babylonian Talmud, *Shabbat* 128b)

If you wound your horse with spurs, you will be ridden in the afterworld by demons whose heel bones are sharpened to spurs. (Bernard Evslin, editor, "The Spirit of Jewish Thought" in *Selections from the Talmud*, Grosset & Dunlap, Inc., New York, 1969, p. 98)

You need only ask the beasts,
And they will teach you;
The birds of the sky,
And they will tell you;
Or speak with the earth,
And it will teach you.
And the fish of the sea
Will tell you stories.
(Job 12:7–8)

Traditional morning prayers begin with a blessing praising God for the rooster. Why? Because its crowing at sunrise wakes you up to the difference between night and day and reminds you to appreciate and take care of God's earth and everything on it. (Philip Birnbaum, editor, *Daily Prayer Book,* Hebrew Publishing Co., New York, 1977, p. 16)

A very important eighteenth-century rabbi was once asked why he spent so much of his time listening to the songs of the birds. "Because," said that famous man, "you can hear in the voice of every bird and beast the voice of God." (Lewis G. Regenstein, *Replenish the Earth,* Crossroad Publishing, New York, 1991, p. 205)

Every kind of fish, bird, and animal contributes something to the world you live in—even the ones you may consider to be unnecessary, such as fleas, gnats, and flies. (*Midrash Genesis Rabbah* 10:7)

III ✦

Torah says:

Care for
the earth.

The earth is your home to cherish and protect.

To the ancient Israelites the earth itself was alive. The environmental laws in the Torah are based on this wisdom. Three thousand years ago the Jews did not have words for the environment and ecology. What they had was the belief that a good life depended on preserving the land. This was a central theme in Judaism. It is expressed today in the celebration of the harvest festivals of Pesach, Shavuot, and Sukot.

✦   ✦   ✦

Your welfare depends on the land just as much as the welfare of the land depends on you.
(Deuteronomy 11:13–17)

One generation goes and one generation comes, but the earth remains forever. (Ecclesiastes 1:4)

Replenish the earth. (Genesis 1:28)

Land, like humans and animals, must have a time of rest to renew itself, says the Torah. Six years you shall plant your field and six years you shall prune your vineyard. But in the seventh year you shall neither plant nor reap. It shall be a year of complete rest for the land. (Leviticus 25:2–5)

In the Bible Adam and Eve were put in the Garden of Eden to "till it and tend it." (Genesis 2:15) This means that caring for the world is every human being's responsibility. (Aubrey Rose, editor, *Judaism and Ecology*, Cassell Publishers Limited, London and New York, 1992, cited by Rabbi Norman Solomon, p. 21)

The world's first environmental law may have been the ancient Judaic commandment *Yishuv Ha'aretz*, which means "Settlement of the Land." This commandment is also called *Yishuv Haolam* or *Tikkun Haolam*, which means "Improving (Repairing) the World."

Not even in times of battle with your enemies do the rulings of the Torah exempt you from caring for the earth. The Torah requires that every foot soldier bury his own excrement (Deuteronomy 23:13–15) and that no food-yielding trees [even those belonging to your enemy] be destroyed. (Deuteronomy 20:19–20)

The Torah says that because you are "made in the image of God" (Genesis 1:27), you are a partner to God in the caretaking of the earth. (Rose, *Judaism and Ecology*, cited by Rabbi Norman Solomon, p. 27)

God's command to humans to "rule the fish of the sea, the birds of the sky, and all the living things that move on the earth" (Genesis 1:28) gave us the responsibility to be the stewards [guardians] of the world. (Lewis G. Regenstein, *Replenish the Earth*, Crossroad Publishing, New York, 1991, pp. 26–27)

The Frog Who
Wanted to Be a Man

Once there was a frog who lived in a marsh pond and wanted nothing more than to be a man. Day after day he bellowed at the sky, "A human! I want to be a human!" Night after night he croaked the same words until all the fish in the sea, all the birds in the sky, and all the animals that walked on the earth were sick of him.

"Oh, God," they pleaded, "please make this frog into a man. Do it for our sake, if not for his."

Finally God took pity on them. "If I choose to let you be a human," God said to the frog, "you must promise to follow faithfully all the laws that I have set forth for people."

"I will! I will!" said the frog, hopping up and down with excitement.

So God changed the frog into a man but ordered a wise old spider to stay with him and help him understand the ways of humans and what God requires of them.

One morning the frog found himself walking along a country road, a spider on his shoulder, although he was unaware of that fact. On his feet were a pair of stiff, very uncomfortable shoes.

Covering his legs was a woolly pair of scratchy pants. Over his chest he wore a shirt with buttons. And on his head was a too-tight brimmed cap.

"Ho, ho!" he said, scratching a bit but still pleased with himself. "Now that I am a human, I will rule the fish of the sea, the birds of the sky, and all the other living things that move on the earth."

"No, you won't," said the spider.

The new man turned around, trying to find the source of the voice.

"As a human," said the spider, "you have a responsibility to protect and preserve the fish of the sea, the birds of the sky, and all the other living things that move on the earth."

The new man didn't understand the meaning of the word "responsibility." He didn't know what "protect" and "preserve" meant, either. But he assumed that they couldn't be too important.

"Oh, well," he said, "what really matters is that I'm a man and not just a thing that swims or flies or creeps or crawls. What matters is that now I, too, look just like God."

"No, you don't," said the spider.

The new man stopped. He turned around again and again but he couldn't see who was talking to him.

Annoyed, he tried to walk rapidly away from the voice. But the spider held on.

"Because you were made in the 'image of God' doesn't mean you *look* like God," the spider continued. "It means you can *be* like God in many ways, if you choose. A flower has only to be a flower, a frog has only to be a frog, but a human can be a partner to God. What you've got to remember is, God is the Creator of the world; humans are its caretakers."

The new man stopped so suddenly that the spider almost fell off his shoulder.

"Who's talking?" he hollered, turning around and around. But he didn't see anyone.

"Me!" shouted the spider, clinging to the new man's shoulder. "It's me!"

The new man looked around again and still saw nobody.

"God?" he asked hesitantly. "Is that you, God?"

The spider started to laugh. "No, you fool. It's me, Spider."

The new man turned his head toward where the sound was coming from. Only then did he see a spider, sitting almost under his chin.

For a brief moment the frog forgot that he was a man. He did what any frog would do. He opened his mouth and quickly swallowed the spider.

And suddenly, everything changed. He was no longer a man walking down a road in the world of humans. Instead, he was sitting on a lily pad in the middle of a marsh pond. He was once again a frog.

He opened his mouth to protest. But all that came out was "ribbit."

The Meaning
of Number Seven

There was once a man who lived in a house so high up on a mountain that he often forgot there was anything more to the world than the sky. He spent his days sleeping and his nights looking at the heavens, keeping track of the stars. So busy was he with the heavens that he knew little of earthly matters.

Daily he supped on a bowl of soup and a piece of bread served to him by the woman who cleaned his house and washed his clothes, but from where the bread and soup came he did not know. Even when he ate, he scribbled numbers on the table-cloth, calculating this and that.

One day he sat down at his kitchen table as usual but no bread and soup were prepared for him.

"Why is this?" he asked.

The good woman who tended to him said, "Sir, my husband has forbidden me to do another chore for you until you leave your house, look around, and see something more than the sky. What you need is a vacation."

"A vacation?" the skygazer repeated. He wasn't sure he knew what a vacation was.

"Here," she said. "I have wrapped a piece of bread and a piece

of cheese and put them into this knapsack. Take it with you and go down the mountain. You'll see what there is to be seen on the earth and learn what there is to be learned."

"A vacation," said the stargazer again, feeling a little bewildered.

But not knowing what else to do, he did what the woman had told him. He left his house and walked down the mountain into the countryside. While he walked, he nibbled at his food. When he had eaten all that the woman had given him, he kept right on walking. He looked neither to the right nor to the left. With no familiar stars to gaze at, he fastened his eyes on his feet.

After a day of walking, he came to a small village. When the villagers saw this strange, hollow-eyed man, they welcomed him. They offered him wine to drink and food to eat. So humble was he and so little did he eat of their food that people began to say this man might be the Messiah.

For days he watched the villagers harvesting wheat and grain from their fields. He had never seen anything like that before.

"How did you make the land give you all that?" he asked the farmers.

"We sowed the seeds," they replied. But the man who had seldom taken his eyes off the heavens didn't know what seeds were.

He watched the villagers going in and out of their houses of study, marching solemnly to their synagogues, and lighting their Sabbath candles.

"Why do you do that?" he asked.

"We are Jews," they told him. "We live by the law of the Torah."

But the words they used had no meaning to him. As they talked, he thought, I, too, could bring wonders out of the ground if I were a Jew.

Whereupon he went to the rabbi. "Rabbi," he said, "I want to be a Jew."

"Hmmmm," said the rabbi. He ushered the man into his house, offered him a chair, and regarded him solemnly.

"Being a Jew," the rabbi started to explain, "means belonging to a people and to a land. The Jewish religion grew out of a special connection between a people and their land."

The man who had spent his life gazing at the heavens leaned forward and listened eagerly.

"The God the Jews pray to requires them to rest on the seventh day," the rabbi continued. "God also requires them to let their fields rest every seventh year and return the fields to their original owners in seven times seven years . . ."

Aha! the stargazer thought. The magic the Jews have over the land lies in the number seven.

"We Jews are also required to leave the corners of our fields for the poor and the hungry . . ."

But the visitor had stopped listening. He was staring at the rabbi without really seeing him. What he was seeing instead was the number seven.

He got up, knocking his chair over in his haste. Mumbling his excuses, he hurriedly left the rabbi's house. He didn't need to become a Jew, he had decided. He'd already learned the secret of the Jews' accomplishments.

Without saying good-bye to anyone, he headed home.

"Seven," he kept whispering to himself. "Seven, seven, and seven times seven." The numbers began spinning around in his head. He gave a little hop, a skip, and something that was very much like a jump. His vacation had been a success. Now all that he had to do, he told himself, was to look into the heavens and find the meaning of number seven.

WHO OWNS WHAT?

TWO MEN ARE FIGHTING OVER A PIECE OF LAND.

THIS IS **MY** LAND!

NO! IT BELONGS TO **ME!**

MINE!

MINE!

FINALLY TO SETTLE THEIR DIFFERENCES, THEY CALL FOR THE RABBI...

AND AGREE TO ABIDE BY HIS DECISION.

THE RABBI LISTENS CAREFULLY FIRST TO ONE...

AND THEN TO THE OTHER.

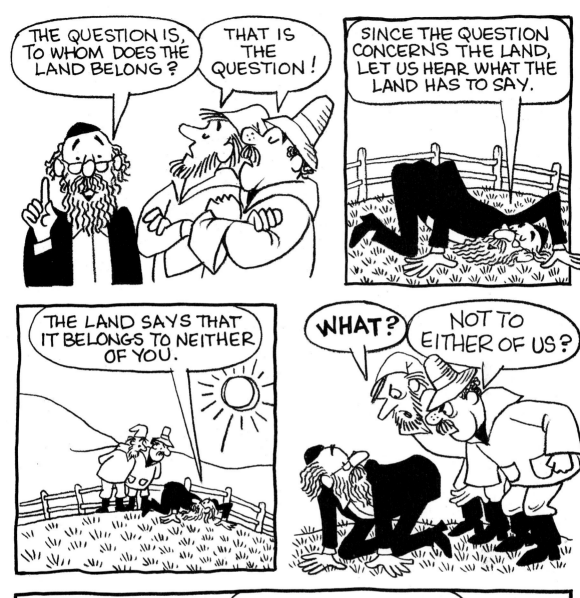

(Chasidic tale, source unknown)

Look upon This Land

Look upon this land—
Touch it.
Sand under your bare feet,
The squish of mud,
Silky coat of cat,
Soft rose petals,
A smooth round rock,
Rain on your face.

Touch it with your eyes.
Cherry trees blossoming pink,
Lake of blue and summer sky,
The green of life,
Purple grapes and apples red,
Moon rising yellow,
Orange sun going down.

Touch it with your ears.
Splatter of rain,
Crack of thunder,
Wind whispering,
Birds singing,
The crying of babies and puppies,
Kittens and ducklings.

Touch it with your nose.
Pine-scent of woods,
Lilacs blooming,
New-mown grass,
Smoke of chimneys,
Strawberries in the sun.

Touch it with your tongue.
Lick of sugar,
Tang of lemon, ginger, or spice,
Bite of cold snow,
Gulp of pure water.

Look upon this land—
Touch it.
Touch it in every way you can,
For this land is part of you,
And you are part of it.

Given into your care is this earth.
See how beautiful it is.
Be careful not to spoil it,
For if you destroy the world,
There will be no one after you to restore it.

(*Midrash Ecclesiastes Rabbah* 1 on Ecclesiastes 7:13)

✦ KEEP IN MIND ✦

The celebration of the earth is heard in many Jewish blessings, prayers, and songs. In Judaism celebrating nature is a way of celebrating God.

Jewish festivals reflect the cycles of the seasons. And Judaic religious symbols are based on nature. It is said that the menorah, a seven-branched candle holder that is a symbol of Jewish life, is patterned after the olive tree. Throughout the world the branch of the olive tree is a symbol of peace.

Woe to the person who stands on the earth and does not see what he or she sees. For in every drop of water in the sea and every grain of dust on the earth is the reflection of God. (Source unknown)

The festival of Sukot began as a celebration of the harvest. Sukot celebrates stewardship—the practice of caring for the earth.

Even a king is subject to the soil—
If the earth yields the produce,
Then a king can accomplish something;
If the earth does not yield,
Then he is of no use whatsoever.
(*Midrash Leviticus Rabbah* 22:1)

IV ✦

Torah says:

Do not
destroy.

Bad things happen when you don't protect what's good.

Human responsibility to the environment is specifically set forth as laws in the Torah. One rabbi counted two hundred mitzvot *or Jewish laws that are concerned with the care of the earth. Probably the most important of these is the law of* Bal Tashchit, *which means "Do Not Destroy." On this law are based the many teachings to respect and conserve all that has been created.*

✦　✦　✦

When you besiege a city for a long time in order to capture it, you must not destroy its trees by wielding an ax against them. You may eat from them, but you must not cut them down.
(Deuteronomy 20:19)

The law of *Bal Tashchit* forbids you to cut down your enemies' fruit trees or to change the course of a stream so that the trees will wither and die. (Maimonides, *Mishneh Torah*, Book of Judges, "Laws of Kings and Wars" 6:8)

Not only a person who cuts down trees that bear fruit or nuts but also anyone who smashes household goods, demolishes a building, stops up a spring, or destroys food transgresses the law of *Bal Tashchit*. (Ibid., 6:10)

Whoever destroys anything that could be useful to others breaks the law of *Bal Tashchit*. (Babylonian Talmud, *Kodashim* 32a)

When God created the first human beings, He led them around the Garden of Eden and said, "See how beautiful the world is! I give it into your care. Do not spoil it. For if you destroy the world, There will be no one after you to restore it." (*Midrash Ecclesiastes Rabbah* 1 on Ecclesiastes 7:13)

Threshing floors must be kept far enough away from a town to prevent the husks of grains and grasses from polluting the air of the town when the wind blows. (*Mishnah Baba Batra* 2:8)

A tannery must be built at least fifty cubits [seventy-five feet] outside a town and must be located only on the east side [downwind] of the town so that foul odors are not carried into the town by the wind. (*Baba Batra* 2:9)

Bury your waste [sewage] away from the area in which people live and bury it deep so that it will not cause harm to anyone walking by. (Deuteronomy 23:13–15; Maimonides, *Mishneh Torah*, "Kings" 6:14–15)

Rabbinic rulings that helped insure a safe and healthy environment included bans against polluting drinking water (*Baba Metzia* 11:31) and against smoke, dust, bad smells, and noise. (*Mishnah Baba Batra*, Chapter 2)

Do not dump waste in any place from which it could be scattered by the wind or spread by flooding. (Maimonides, *Mishneh Torah*, "Tamid and Musaf Offerings" 2:15)

Furnaces and other causes of smoke, odor, and air pollution are not permitted inside a city. (*Baba Kamma* 82b)

The Man Who Walked
in God's Shoes

There was once a young and very earnest farmer who loved the beauty of summer and hated the dreariness of winter. When the flowers bloomed and the fruit ripened and the birds sang, he would dance in his fields and praise God loudly and frequently. But when the earth was swept by rain and hail and wind, he would shake his fist at the sky, go into his house, and sit grumbling by the fire.

"Listen to me, God!" he shouted on one particularly cold and rainy day. "If You are so powerful, why can't the flowers bloom all year around? Why can't the fruit be ripe forever? Why do You let the leaves fall and the trees stand bare all winter long? Why must there be death and darkness? Oh, God, if I were only in Your shoes, what glories I would perform!"

Suddenly he found himself being shaken.

"Wake up! Wake up!" his wife was shouting in his ear. "You're yelling in your sleep again."

The farmer opened his eyes, pushed himself out of his chair, and stood up.

"For heaven's sake!" his wife said. "What are you wearing on your feet?"

He looked down. On his feet were silk sandals, the kind that only lords wear.

Cautiously the farmer took a few steps. He stamped his feet. He jumped up and down. The sandals were still there, clinging to his feet.

When he told his wife that he was wearing God's shoes, she didn't believe him.

Looking at his feet, he said slowly and clearly, "Let there be light! Let the leaves stay on the trees and the rain and the cold disappear from the earth!"

Immediately the room became bright with sunshine. The farmer's wife rushed to the window. The sky that had hung low and dark was blue and cloudless. The tree that had stood with naked branches was blooming right before their eyes.

"Let the grain always be golden," he shouted, "and the fruit be ripe forever."

Suddenly the fields of grain were full and yellow, although it was still the middle of winter. The trees were laden with fruit. The gardens teemed with ripe vegetables. Flowers were blooming everywhere.

Never had the people seen such abundance. They burst out of their houses and started to sing in the streets.

"My husband is doing God's work," the farmer's wife explained again and again.

Long lines of people began to form to inspect the earnest farmer's silk shoes and to receive his blessing. And because the crops continued to yield and the flowers continued to bloom through the passing seasons, the people began to call the farmer Mister and Master and Lord.

By his decree, nothing died—not flowers, not trees, not plants, not even weeds.

As time went by, the farmer became more and more lordly. Every morning he strutted up and down the streets in his silk shoes, inspecting his domain.

"The earth is God's and the fullness that comes from it," he kept reminding everybody.

People made way for him as he passed and bowed their heads, thanking him for all the good things that he had done for them on the earth.

But early one morning his wife shook him awake with a great shout.

"What's the matter?" he cried.

"I harvested the wheat, threshed the grain, ground it into flour, and baked my bread. But alas! When I took the bread out of the oven, it fell to pieces!" she sobbed.

The farmer picked up a piece of bread and tasted it.

"Pooey!" he said and spit it out. It tasted like cotton.

He then picked up a pitcher of goat's milk from the table and took a long drink.

"Yuuuuch!" he cried, wiping his mouth. It tasted like sour water.

He grabbed an apple and took a bite but just as quickly spit it out. The apple tasted like sand, an orange tasted like vinegar, a potato like mud.

Cries arose from every house, every field, every orchard, and every barn. From everywhere people were screaming at the farmer who wore God's shoes and had deceived them with his false blessings.

"What have you done? What have you done?" his wife cried in terror.

The frightened man raised his voice to the heavens. "Dear God! What have I done? What have I done?"

The voice of God boomed loud inside his head, "What you have done is discover a truth."

The words banged against the farmer's ears. They passed through his body so quickly that his knees gave way beneath him. His teeth began to chatter. "A—a what?"

"A truth that has been the way of the earth since the beginning of time," the voice continued.

"What is the truth that I have discovered?" cried the terrified farmer.

"The truth," said the voice of God, "is that death and decay and darkness are necessary parts of birth and life and light.

"Petals and leaves must fade, dry up, and fall. They must decay to help nourish the earth. Only then can new seeds and new life grow."

The farmer's mouth fell open as he listened.

"Destroy the natural order of the earth and sooner or later you will destroy all living things," said the voice before it completely faded away.

The man who had walked in the shoes of God looked down and saw that his feet were bare. He was no longer wearing God's shoes.

Thankfully he rose and went out of his house.

The rain fell on his head. The leaves swirled around his feet.

The grain withered and the flowers drooped.

The darkness of winter had returned.

"Praise God!" the farmer shouted. For all was once again as it should be on God's earth.

(Based on Martin Buber's story "The Angel and the World's Dominion" in *Tales of Angels, Spirits & Demons*, Hawks Well Press, New York, 1958)

The Inheritance

Once there was a woman who married a widower with three sons. They cared nothing for the land that their father loved, paying little attention to what he tried to teach them. Wasteful and lazy, they simply threw away everything that they had no immediate use for. After all, what did it matter?

"It matters a lot," their father told them. "Nothing that is thrown away ever really *goes* away."

They only laughed at his words.

"There's no place on the earth that's not part of every other place," their father tried to explain. "Everything is connected."

The sons winked at one another behind their father's back. They plainly thought that the old man took everything too seriously.

When the woman's husband suddenly died, she decided to teach the sons a lesson they needed to learn.

One day she called them together and said, "Your father has left something to you well worth its weight in gold. It will be given to you in exactly one year and one day from now. But in order to get it, you must each first go back to your house and throw away whatever you find on the doorstep.

"The only requirement is that what you do with what you find must leave no effect, either good or bad, on anything else.

In other words, your task is to remove what you find as thoroughly as if it had never been on the face of the earth."

The sons grinned at one another. Each was already planning how to spend his unexpected fortune.

Upon returning to his house, the first son found a bucket of dead fish on his doorstep. Holding his nose, he carried the bucket out to the backyard and buried it.

The second son went home and found a barrel of lamp oil sitting in front of his door. Without wasting time or giving the matter any thought, he rolled the barrel to the street, poured the oil down the drain, and watched it trickle away. Then he smashed the barrel and tossed the pieces into the running stream at the bottom of the hill behind his house.

The third son found a wheelbarrow of containers filled with something guaranteed to kill rats, mice, snails, and bugs. He scratched his head as he regarded the stuff. Then, having

thought of an easy solution, he laughed. He trudged down the street pushing the wheelbarrow in front of him until he reached a deserted old barn. Climbing up a ladder on the outside of the barn, he emptied the containers onto the scattered hay that had been left on the barn floor below and nailed some boards over the opening. After tossing the containers into an abandoned well, he returned home.

When the year and a day had passed, the three sons hastened to the home of their father's wife and held out their hands for their inheritance.

"Wait," said their father's widow. "First I must see whether or not all the conditions have been met."

Then the clever woman went to visit each son's house in turn.

At the first son's house a bush had grown where the dead fish had been buried.

At the second son's house it seemed at first as if the oil had disappeared with no trace at all—until a child appeared crying because the water in the nearby stream had been polluted and all the fish had died.

At the third son's house a crowd had gathered. It seemed that some children who had been exploring an old barn nearby had found it filled with dead birds. And a man who lived near the well was claiming that poisoned water had contaminated the soil in his vegetable garden.

Protesting that they were not responsible for any of these things, the three sons took the woman to the rabbi.

"Since one result was good and two were bad," concluded the rabbi after listening to the whole story, "it can't be said that you fulfilled the requirement to neither benefit nor harm anything."

"It's impossible to get rid of anything without affecting anything else!" shouted the first son. "It can't be done! Not by us, not by anyone!"

"Why not?" asked the rabbi mildly.

"Because everything on the earth is connected to everything else . . ." replied the second son.

"You can't throw anything away because there is no *away!*" said the third.

Then the woman spoke up. "Rabbi, what would you say such conclusions are worth?"

"They're worth their weight in gold, and more," answered the rabbi.

"I think," said the woman to her husband's sons, "that each of you has just received your rightful inheritance."

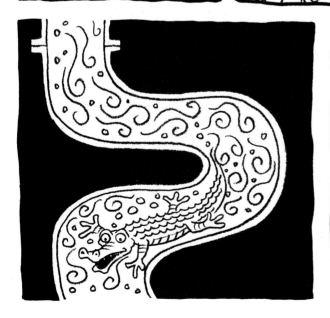

ONE YEAR LATER

TWO YEARS LATER

THREE YEARS LATER

SIX YEARS LATER

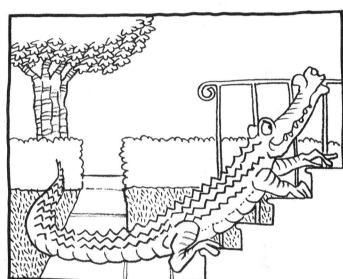

(Based on a parable in the Babylonian Talmud, *Baba Kamma* 50b)

✦ KEEP IN MIND ✦

The Creator who formed the earth and made it did not create it a waste but formed it for habitation. (Isaiah 45:18)

If you drop a bottle on a street and go away without picking up the pieces, you are breaking the law of *Bal Tashchit*. (*Baba Kamma* 30a)

Major General Avraham Yaffee, an Israeli tank commander, once ordered an entire encampment to pull up stakes and move to another location in order to avoid the trampling and destruction of a field of rare wild flowers.

Another time the major general halted his tank and ordered a cease-fire to allow a rare bird, a cream-colored courser, to cross the path and move out of harm's way. (Lewis G. Regenstein, *Replenish the Earth*, Crossroad Publishing, New York, 1991, p. 213)

V ✦

Torah says:

All living
things are
connected.

Every living thing on the earth
is part of everything else.

Judaism does not separate people from nature. Rabbis teach that the earth, with all its different kinds of plants, trees, birds, fish, beasts, and people, is a unit of one, just as God is One. Whatever affects the families of plant and animal life on the earth affects the families of humans, too. This is repeated throughout the teachings of the Torah: If we destroy the other kinds of living things on the earth, we will destroy ourselves.

◆　◆　◆

When we say the *Shema*, that God is One (Deuteronomy 6:4), we are saying that everything and everyone is connected . . . all are part of the same One. (Lawrence Kushner, *The Book of Miracles*, UAHC Press, New York, 1987, p. 19)

The whole world of humans, animals, fish, and birds all depend on one another. All drink the earth's water, breathe the earth's air, and find their food in what was created on the earth. All share the same destiny. (*Tanna de Bei Eliyahu Rabbah 2*)

What happens to the sons and
daughters of men and women
also happens to beasts . . .
as one dies, so dies the other;
all share the same breath of life.
(Ecclesiastes 3:19)

Every living thing remains, even
in death, very much a part of the
web of life. After a living thing
dies, its remains provide
nutrients for the soil. From this
soil a tree may grow, which
provides fruit for a human or a
home to an owl, etc. (Ellen
Bernstein and Dan Fink, *Let the
Earth Teach You Torah*, Shomrei
Adamah/Keepers of the Earth,
Pennsylvania, 1992, p. 80)

Judaism teaches that what you do today affects what the world
will be like tomorrow. Each generation is linked to the next by
its actions. We depend on those who came before us, just as our
children will depend on us. (Kushner, *The Book of Miracles*, p. 17)

Robber! Robber!

A tale is told of a pious man who returned to his home after a journey to find that all he valued in life had been destroyed by a fire.

He spent his days mourning for what he had lost and his nights shouting blame at God. But no matter how loud he shouted, there was no sign that God was listening.

Convinced that the Creator had no connection with any living thing on the earth, the man vowed that he would never pray again. Determined to turn his back on all that he had believed in, he set out to begin a new life.

When he had walked until he was too tired and hungry to go any farther, he came upon a tree laden with fruit by the side of the road. Seeing no one around, he greedily feasted on the fruit of the tree. He then sat down to rest and fell asleep.

Suddenly he heard, "Robber, robber, robber!"

Sleeping fitfully, he turned first one way and then the other.

"Robber, robber, robber!" he heard again.

He muttered in his sleep, explaining that he had done only what any hungry traveler would have. Besides, taking fruit from a roadside tree wasn't exactly stealing. And no real harm had been done. But the voice didn't stop.

"Robber, robber, robber!"

The man didn't wake up. Suddenly he felt a sting on his shoulder. "Go away," he muttered.

The stinging continued. He slapped at the spot.

"You shouldn't have done that." It was only a whisper, but he heard it. He heard it clearly.

He dreamed that he opened his eyes.

"Who said that?" he asked.

A breath fluttered over his face. He smelled the whiff of apple blossoms. He dreamed that he sat up, looked around, and saw no one.

"Who are you? Where are you?" he asked again.

"You don't know it, but you're talking to an angel," he heard a voice say. "And I'm sitting right here up in this tree."

The man laughed. He laughed out loud in his sleep. This dream was really ridiculous. But he was too tired to care.

"You'd better believe me. It's nothing to laugh about," said the voice.

The man decided to pretend the dream was real. "What kind of an angel are you anyway?" he asked.

"The guardian kind."

"You're not *my* guardian angel, are you?"

The angel hooted. "Of course not. I'm an apple tree angel."

"I never heard of that kind of angel," the man replied.

"Obviously," the angel said. "Every fruit tree has a guardian angel who is responsible for it."

"I can assure you," said the traveler, pulling his coin purse from his pocket, "I'm quite willing to pay for the apples I ate."

"Humans are sometimes so dumb," the angel said. "You can't *pay* me for them. Every fruit of every tree holds a spark of God's energy in it. If a blessing is not said over a fruit before it is eaten, that spark is lost and the tree cannot produce another fruit to replace it. It's not the money I'm worried about, it's the *shefa*."

"*Shefa*?" the man repeated.

The word echoed and reechoed in the man's head, but the angel said no more. Oh, well, the traveler thought, it was only a dream. He sighed, turned over, and went back to sleep. He slept for a long time.

He dreamed that he slept for a year and a day, awoke, stretched, yawned, and felt ravenously hungry. He saw himself looking up into the tree, rubbing his eyes, and looking up again.

While he was asleep, the tree had grown. It had grown as much as it would have grown in a whole year's time. But the branch from which the man had taken the apples was bare. It had reproduced no fruit at all.

"I told you!" the voice of the angel accused him. "No *shefa*."

Suddenly the man understood. By not saying a blessing over

70

the fruit he had eaten, he had robbed the branch of its spark of God.

Carefully he plucked an apple from another branch. But before he bit into it, he closed his eyes and said: *Baruch Atah Adonai Elohenu Melech haolam borei peri haetz.* "Blessed are You our God, Ruler of the universe, Creator of the fruit of the tree."

When the man opened his eyes, there was no apple in his hand and no angel in the tree. He was lying on the ground. Sitting up slowly, he rose to his feet and brushed the grass and twigs from his clothes. Then he stood for a long moment looking up into the apple tree.

"Thank You, God," he said finally and started back the way he had come.

(Adapted from a story in the Kabbalah)

The Visitor

It is said that the Keeper of the Earth was once visited by a traveler from Space. Wanting to be a good host, the Keeper of the Earth showed the visitor around.

She showed her the mountains and the seas, the rivers and the streams, the forests and the fields, the wondrous colored flowers and the sweet-tasting fruits. She introduced the guest to the Lion, the King of Beasts; the Eagle, the King of Birds; the Salmon, the King of Fish; and the Bee, the Queen of Insects.

"Oh, my!" said the visitor. "You have so much of everything." And she told the Keeper of the Earth how meager her own place in Space was, how thin the air, how dark the atmosphere, how bare of fruits and flowers and birds.

"How happy I would be," she said, "if you would give me only one of the earth's many riches. Surely you do not need them all."

The Keeper of the Earth gave the visitor a polite smile. "Show me what is not needed here," she said, "and I promise you that it will be yours."

The visitor from Space instantly agreed. She decided to ask for a small thing—something not very important so that her host would look upon her request with favor. The visitor's reasoning was that the next time she would ask for something bigger and

the next time something even bigger than before. Soon, she cal-
culated, she would be the Ruler of the Earth as well as of Space.

So the visitor from Space chose something very small. "Butterflies," she said. "Let the butterflies go with me into Space. There
they would have plenty of room to fly around and show off their
beautiful wings."

"But if I give you the butterflies," said the Keeper of the Earth,
"who would spread the pollen from flower to flower? Without
butterflies, there would be no flowers. And without flowers,
there would be no nectar for the bees and without bees . . ."

Impatiently the visitor held up her hand to stop the Keeper of
the Earth. She fixed her attention on a row of tiny green plants.
If she took them, she thought, all the flowers would follow.
Then the butterflies would come, too. She congratulated herself
on her cleverness.

"Dear Keeper of the Earth, give me only these very small
green plants," she requested. "Surely they would not be missed."

The Keeper of the Earth smiled at the visitor from Space. "If I were to give you the green plants, what would turn the sunlight into food energy? Without green plants, all the insects would die of starvation. If the insects died, the tadpoles and the other small creatures that feed on the insects would also die. And if they died, the fish and birds that feed on them would die, too, and if . . ."

With a screech that tore a hole in the sky above the earth, the traveler from Space clapped her hands over her ears and took herself back to her own world.

(Based on a parable in *Midrash Leviticus Rabbah* 4:6, which compares a boat and its passengers to the world and its inhabitants)

✦ KEEP IN MIND ✦

The universe whispers that all things are intertwined. (Chaim Stern, editor, *Gates of Prayer*, CCAR, New York, 1975, p. 221)

✦   ✦   ✦

One who thinks he can live without others is mistaken. One who thinks others cannot live without him is more mistaken. (Bernard Evslin, editor, "The Spirit of Jewish Thought" in *Selections from the Talmud*, Grosset & Dunlap, Inc., New York, 1969, p. 102)

Jewish mystics believed that the outer world of nature is a mirror of people's inner nature. They believed that the more you learn about nature, the more you'll know about yourself.

A very old legend tells how closely all things are connected. The legend says that when God created the world, each fruit tree produced many different kinds of fruit. Apples, peaches, pears, and plums could all be picked from one tree. But when Cain killed his brother, Abel, the full strength of the trees was killed, too. From that day on, each tree yielded only one kind of fruit.

(Adapted by permission from *Seder Tu Bishvat: The Festival of Trees*, CCAR, New York, 1989)

Some Things to Know

Aggadah: Stories, examples, parables, and other such nonlegal material found in the Midrash, Talmud, and other rabbinic literature.

Ecology: The study of the earth. The term comes from *ecos*, a Greek word that means "house," and the Greek word *ology*, which means "study." Therefore, ecology is the study of the earth as your home.

Environment: Everything that surrounds a living thing and affects the way in which it grows or develops.

The Five Books of Moses: Also known as the Torah. The Five Books are (1) Genesis; (2) Exodus; (3) Leviticus; (4) Numbers; and (5) Deuteronomy.

Gemara: The second section of the Talmud. The *Gemara* is a commentary on the *Mishnah*. It is a collection of discussions and decisions on both legal and general issues made by notable scholars (called *amoraim*, which means "interpreters") who lived in Palestine and Babylon before 500 C.E.

Halachah: Jewish law.

Hebrew Bible (or *Tanach*): Known in the Christian world as the Old Testament. It has three parts: the Torah, the Prophets, and the Writings.

Kabbalah: Jewish mysticism, which can be traced to ancient times in Palestine and Babylonia. In the seventh to ninth centuries, specific works on mysticism were published.

Midrash: To "search" or "investigate." The Midrash consists of interpretations of biblical texts that explain or illustrate the laws and principles of the Torah through stories, legends, and anecdotes.

Mishnah: The first section of the Talmud. The *Mishnah* is a guide to action or conduct that was put into written form in about 200 C.E. The *Mishnah* discusses and explains laws that have to do with problems in people's work, their community, and their religious lives.

Parashah: A Torah portion that is read or chanted each week, or a selection from a portion.

Rabbah: "The Great." *Rabbah* is added to a title of an important book or collection of books, for example, *Midrash Rabbah,* "The Great Midrash."

Sefer Torah: A scroll of the Torah from which a *parashah* (portion) is chanted or read. A *Sefer Torah* is written on pages of parchment by a trained scribe or *sofer.*

Shofetim (or *Shoftim*): The Book of Judges.

Siddur: A Jewish prayer book containing the daily prayers.

Sifra: The halachic *midrash* to the Book of Leviticus.

Sifre: A collection of stories and interpretations based on the Books of Numbers and Deuteronomy.

Talmud: A record of Jewish lore and law. It is made up of the *Mishnah* and the *Gemara*. The Jerusalem Talmud is the edition that was produced in Palestine in 400 C.E. It combines the *Mishnah* and the Jerusalem *Gemara*. The larger Babylonian Talmud was produced in Babylonia in 500 C.E. It combines the *Mishnah* and the Babylonian *Gemara*.

Torah: A term that is commonly used to mean the entire body of Jewish wisdom, including the Five Books of Moses (specifically called the Torah), the Prophets, the Writings, the Midrash, the Talmud, and other rabbinic commentaries.

The Torah (or the Teaching): The first five books of the Hebrew Bible. It tells of the covenant between God and Israel and the commandments that the covenant prescribes. The Torah is also known as the Five Books of Moses. It tells the history of the Jewish people from the time of Creation to the death of Moses.

Tosefta: A supplement to the *Mishnah*.

Torah Tree

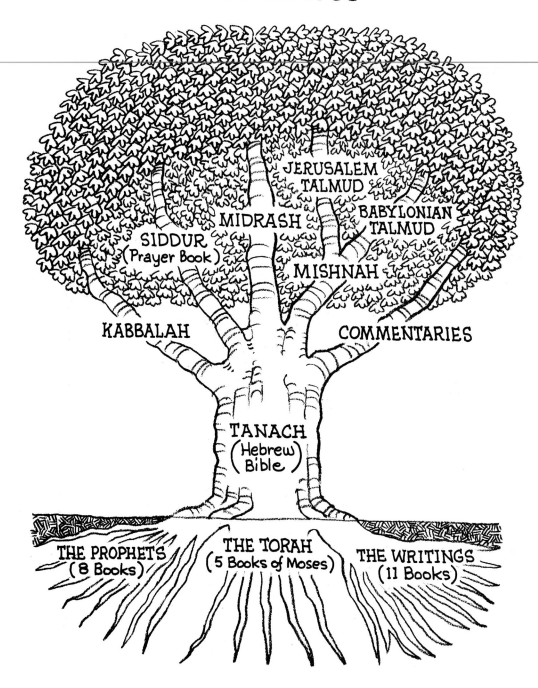

✦ BLESSINGS ✦

Blessings are reminders that the beauty of nature and the abundance of the fruit on the earth are all part of God's world. Blessings also remind us that this world is in our care.

✦　✦　✦

If you enjoy something in this world without first saying a blessing, it is as if you stole it. (Babylonian Talmud, *Berachot* 35a–b)

Say this blessing on seeing the first trees in blossom:

Baruch Atah Adonai
Elohenu Melech haolam
shelo chisar beolamo davar
uvara vo beriyot tovot
veilanot tovim lehanot
bachem benei adam.

Blessed are You our God,
Ruler of the universe,
whose world lacks nothing
needful and who has fashioned
goodly creatures and lovely
trees that human beings can
enjoy.

Say this blessing on tasting the first fruit of the season:

Baruch Atah Adonai
Elohenu Melech haolam
shehecheyanu
vekiyemanu
vehigianu lazeman hazeh.

Blessed are You our God,
Ruler of the universe,
for giving us life,
for sustaining us,
and for enabling us to
reach this moment.

Say this blessing when you smell a pleasant scent from grasses and from trees. (There are five different blessings for various kinds of such fragrances):

(For grasses)
Baruch Atah Adonai   Blessed are You our God,
Elohenu Melech haolam Ruler of the universe,
borei isvu vesamim.   for all the fragrant grasses.

(For trees)
borei atzei vesamim.   for all the fragrant
           trees.

Say this blessing before eating the fruit of the tree:

Baruch Atah Adonai   Blessed are You our God,
Elohenu Melech haolam Ruler of the universe,
borei peri haetz.   Creator of the fruit of the
           tree.

Acknowledgments

To write a book for young readers on the subject of the environmental wisdom inherent in Judaic teachings was the suggestion of UAHC editor Aron Hirt-Manheimer. I thank him for the help, encouragement, interest, and enthusiasm he provided me with throughout every phase of my research and writing.

For the careful critiques of the manuscript during its final stages, which were invaluable in helping me bring it to its present form, my thanks to: Rabbi Norman Hirsh, Temple Beth Am, Seattle, WA; Rabbi Robert Orkland, Temple Israel, Westport, CT; Rabbi Daniel Swartz, Religious Action Center, Washington, D.C.; and Rabbi Bernard Zlotowitz, Senior Scholar, UAHC. Also my thanks to Kathy Parnass for her outstanding copyediting.

In addition to the traditional Judaic sources, the following sources were especially helpful to me in preparing material for this manuscript: A *Garden of Choice Fruit* edited by David E. Stein, Shomrei Adamah/Keepers of the Earth; *Judaism and Ecology* edited by Aubrey Rose, Cassell Publishers Limited; *Replenish the Earth* by Lewis G. Regenstein, Crossroad Publishing Company; *Preserving Our Environment through the Prism of Rabbinic Literature* by Rabbi Norman Cohen, Central Synagogue, New York City; *Let the Earth Teach You Torah* by Ellen Bernstein and Dan Fink, Shomrei Adamah/Keepers of the Earth; and *A Book of Miracles* by Lawrence Kushner, UAHC Press.